For ALL Combat Wounds

Aaron Michael Grant

CONTENTS

Put the knife down...put the gun down and just read

★★★★★

Make no mistake, you feel alone. You have no hope and have no way out. You find joy in nothing. All is meaningless in a place you'd kill just to feel. You want to hurt yourself because you want to feel something - anything. You want to have control over something, *anything*. Everything is completely screwed up; everybody is screwed up - so what's the damn point? "What does it matter if I disappear? At least then it's all over, and I will have no more pain."

Or maybe you think that your best days are behind you. Your best was long ago, and you'll never be that perfect again. You were doing something important there, and you *hate* domestic life. No one understands that you don't give a crap about groceries, dinner parties, or the color of curtains. Who gives a damn about the height of the lawn and neighborhood gossip! It doesn't matter! None of it matters! Only life and death matters, and they know nothing! Your flag and honors are on the wall, and they don't seem to give a damn. Maybe they'd care, maybe they'd notice if you were gone. Then they would realize what they lost. Why does it feel good to think like this?

Or maybe you feel unwanted. The older you get the more people take advantage of you, and suddenly no one is left that cares. They die or drift away, and all of the sudden, you are forty years old and completely alone.

Your feelings don't lie. No one can tell you different. But there is one thing you must know:

You **are** needed. **You** are the veteran they will turn to in a crisis. What do you think they will do if something goes bad? All eyeballs will fix on you in *complete trust*. You are the veteran that will save them. You are the one that represents them. You are the one that protects them. Who else will? Who else has been where you've been? Who else has seen what you've seen? They are **not** better off without you. **You** are their champion. Take it. Claim it. Honor yourself and honor them by staying prepared.

Yes, they don't realize the full measure of your devotion. You suffer every day, and they don't notice, or hardly give you a second thought - but they can't read minds. They have no idea you are fighting in the desert or fighting in Vietnam. They cannot know what it is to be you, but they can learn to understand silence. And it is silence that kills.

They need you. America needs you. Your job is not over.

Semper Parati

Counting The Cost

In 2014, a veteran of the Iraq War took his own life. His name: Jimmy Kalitz. He was a jokester in our platoon. When you looked at him you never really knew what he was going to do next. It was partly humor. His perfect poker face split at the right moment and all around him roared in laughter. Some bent over and wheezed, some could scarcely breathe. And part of that humor was that he spoke the truth - even if it was ridiculous or contraband, even if it was detrimental to those about, and even if it was not appropriate. He had a way with men because he said what needed to be said, even if an officer were present. What he said was always the truth in humor or otherwise, and the marines loved him for it. Somehow, he always got away with it, perhaps because the truth stuck, perhaps because any that challenged it would end up with egg on their face. We didn't know each other well, but we shared a barracks room, and we shared a drink more than once too. I hadn't spoken to him in fifteen years, and I knew little of his situation, but nonetheless, he was gone.

Some call it the "mark of Cain" where killing men leaves a scar. For us it was the Iraq War: 2003. We were barely twenty years old - but *this* was different. *This* was closer. It was somehow more real. Kalitz left behind a few young girls, *very* young girls. Now they had no father - now they would be on their own. We all felt so helpless. Flowers didn't feel like enough. Silence seemed to be the best therapy for many days. Then, so many questions. "Maybe if I had done this or that he'd still be alive. Maybe if I helped more, maybe if I called more, cared more. And why…why is it always the jokester that hurts the most inside?" Was it the mark of war that caused all of it?

A few years later it was another marine: Russell Chiacchia. This one really hit home. Another jokester in the platoon, he loved to party. Chills went down my spine when I found out he died in his sleep on his 40th birthday. It might have been suicide, but no one really knew. He had *young* daughters and grandkids too. Grandkids at forty. Though I was thankful to still be young without them; *he* had them - *he* was a grandpa, and now he was gone. Then all the "maybes" came back. "Maybe I should have done this or that. Maybe I should have called more, done more, cared more." And the *why* – a fifty-ton loaded question with endless dead-ends. I just spoke to him on the phone – gone. We shared a barracks together for *years*, spent many weekends together, and even got into a couple of scuffles. We were expert riflemen, then we became range coaches together teaching thousands of marines to shoot. He and Kalitz were in Iraq too in the same company. He is in many photos. So many photos.

The photo album of the war was taken down and worshipped. There he is. Young, and tough as nails. All the pictures were happy. No one really takes pictures of negative things, though they do exist. No - these were happy pictures. One day in 2001, the squad lined up as I beat them all, one by one, arm-wrestling until I was exhausted. I was undefeated. I was still undefeated when he sat opposite and 'beat' me after I was worn out. Everyone roared - I still won. There he is again on my 19th birthday. There was nothing to do that night in Fort Knox, Kentucky and Private First Class Rus somehow found out it was my birthday. I tried to keep it secret because I knew what would happen. While I was in the bathroom he schemed and readied the ambush. My hand was on the knob, and I could hear whispers - he was *really bad* at this. So, I decided to play along and act surprised. The door swung open, and they were standing there like idiots with duct tape. I exhaled, "ok let's get this over wi...." I exhaled, "ok let's get this over wi..." The light was swatted off to a pitch-black ruckus.

Now, hazing was not allowed in the Marine Corps, but it happened all the time. This time it was fun though, because when the light went off, I leapt on Rus and surprised all of them: tall guy gets knocked over by the tiny one. Five on one. I don't know how they found my camera, but someone snapped a picture as I was getting taped up. One picture, I thwarted all of them and ripped free, another I was head locked. I threw two of them on the cold vinyl, and another - they finally got wise and hit me all at once. Duct taped and exhausted, he presented me with a fine bottle of scotch; contraband in the barracks, and it was quickly consumed by all of us. That's where he gave me the name: *Mighty Mouse*. He also nicknamed me *Ball-of-Fire* when they watched me down scotch whisky without a flinch. Early the next morning he shook his head when I did twenty-two pullups after a night like that. The five-mile run after made some of us puke. Not me though. I was immune to scotch. "Ball-of-Fire" he smiled. In six months, we graduated tank school and never looked back. There he is lined up with all the other marines in camouflaged utilities. We all looked the same: excited, and scared to death of our sergeants. Now he was gone.

Maybe if I called him more. Maybe if he didn't live so far away. Maybe I should have made time to visit. Maybe this...maybe that...

More silence and the pages turned.

Boy, did we have good times then. During my first two years in the corps, I spent most of my time with Russel on and off duty. Late nights and long days. Good times, and bad times. He was right behind me in Iraq crammed in the long line of tanks up to Baghdad on highway 1. While I was fighting north, he had somehow found time to visit Babylon and the brilliant blue Ishtar Gate. I was filled with jealousy when he got ahold of one of the "Saddam bricks" with the tyrant's face upon it and brought it home as proof. And though it had been twenty years since, he was only forty years old **with** granddaughters. I had *just* spoken to him. I had *just* gotten a text. Gone.

Another picture of some field in Camp Lejeune, North Carolina. My jeep was covered in mud after hitting the biggest puddle I had ever seen. A minute before we sat and idled, and there was no easy way around. For all we knew it might be five feet deep. He didn't expect it when I slammed it in gear and shouted like a crazy person as we hit the water **hard**. I had never heard Russ make that kind of noise before. It was a forced laugh and a screech, and the muddy water shot up our noses like a wall and took out the sunlight. All of it crashed onto the open top and we were utterly filthy. We had never laughed so hard. What a day that was! Nasty.

More pages. More silence.

Something had to be done. If I closed the memories, if I closed the book and did nothing it would compound. Two gone, then it would be three. Then five and ten. I would send letters and flowers, but it wasn't enough. What else could I do? Could I accept **that** and do nothing? No. Something had to be done...but what? What could one man do about thousands out there who daily skirt suicide?

But what the hell was happening?! What was suicide? What was this thing that was killing the men I served with?

Life tends to make us lose contact and take old friends for granted. Especially men, and especially marines. We compartmentalize the past in our minds and don't reach out. We are used to **not** asking for anything and it becomes our way of living. We can easily contact one another who are sometimes only a few hours away, but we don't - we take each other for granted. 'He'll be there if I need him. He'll be there if I want to visit,' we tell the backburner of our minds. Then life gets in the way, and we hate ourselves for not doing better.

Being better. I knew in my heart Jim and Russ wouldn't be the last. I knew I would live through many more, and though I made a solemn vow to not take my friends for granted, I knew more would come. More would definitely come.

Over 141,000 veterans have committed suicide since September 11th, 2001.

When I read the number, I didn't speak for an hour. These veterans had the best care *in the world.* They had the Veterans Administration; a government entity that has *vastly* improved since Vietnam. They had clear access to physicians, psychologists, and psychiatrists. They could call the 988-crisis line if they were suicidal anytime, and even talk to a veteran… yet they were still dying. Well over half of those who committed suicide were veterans who had seen combat. Nearly 70% had been through hell, and it hadn't stopped right up to the day they died. They knew the adrenaline rush of combat, and like them, every moment of my life became measured by an hour in time. A week in time. A war in time. A prison of the mind - dark and unseen like the days they suffer. Veterans keep quiet about war because it is duty to keep it. To keep silent. Not one ounce of hell ought to be dropped in the ears of those we love. THAT is duty. It is a hard sort of honor, but honor, nonetheless.

America is losing her finest because they feel they have no way out - because they have had enough - because they are at the end of their rope and choose suicide. They could have an amazing day then want to die the next morning. They could have a great month then want to die the next minute. It could be no other reason than to just be done with it all. To just have peace. Yes - the rollercoaster is real. What can America do to kill suicide?

But *something* had to be done. It was on the news everywhere. Everyone spoke of twenty-two suicides a day, and no one provided a real solution. How could they? Most spoke of services. "The veterans need more services, and fewer will die. They need homes, jobs, therapy; they need money." I heard it all. Then there were some that wanted to overhaul the whole VA system, and there are always those that want heads to roll. But none of these things would have saved my friends. They would not have saved me either. There was something just under the surface. There was something just outside reach that required prayer. And the more the Almighty pushed me to it, the more committed I became to figuring it out; I looked inward and asked plainly, like I was a split personality: "What do **you** need to keep moving? What do you **need** to stay alive? What do you need to **thrive**?" The answer was simple yet difficult. To stagnate was to die. To do nothing was to die. But it was obvious: American veterans must conquer the darkness to stay alive. But how?

It was found among worms. In the garden I was at peace. Sweaty peace with snakes and black soil, it was easy to talk to my Creator. The helpless plants needed me, and they needed Him where I gave the labor, and He gave the increase. In the presence of worms, I was hit. It was so simple, so elemental, and it was **not** going to be easy. Simple yet difficult - requiring a *lifetime* commitment. I sent up a prayer. I wish I could remember the words.

I found it on my knees in the garden - *it was about the soul.*

Honor. Veterans need to be honored; otherwise, why would he choose death over life? I was lucky, I had a wife and a family who honored me; but many did not. I could hardly imagine a life where no one knew of my war or the sword on our mantle. It was nearly beyond imagination that I could have *no legacy.* And THAT is the heart of the matter: honoring legacy. No one wants to be forgotten. No veteran *wants* to be forgotten. They want to be honored, revered, appreciated - there is no other way to bring a soul back from the darkness than to give him these things, and the surest way was to *tangibly* recognize them. Something tangible for an intangible soul. *Something to show America is with veterans even in the darkest hours.* Yes, they need to be honored.

Memorial Day

★★★★★

In 2018, I was honored to bestow the Purple Heart on a veteran from the Vietnam War. Normally an officer and the highest-ranking enlisted man bestows the medal soon after the wound was made. But *that* day, long after Vietnam, I was staff non-commissioned officer **alone**. It was Memorial-Day in middle of nowhere New York, and I was asked to make a speech in the Naples village square. Somehow, outside all odds, though I had been honorably discharged for eight years, I dawned the old uniform and it still fit! I rehearsed a speech for weeks, and finished it in front of the whole town. Somehow, I had no idea what *legacy* meant until that moment - a moment that burned into my mind. The Purple Heart was warm in-hand. The lives of three veterans were about to change forever.

"Memorial Day is about the veterans who never made it home. We lay flowers on graves in remembrance of those who gave *everything* for complete strangers - for **You**. That's what Memorial Day is all about."

Then they really needed to *see* the Purple Heart – so I showed them. In the white glove of my hand, I paced through the hundreds of faces and children who had never seen the medal before. It took a long few minutes to show everyone, but it was worth it. Then I made my way back to the front. The honor guard full of veterans were ready to do a 21-gun salute the moment my speech ended.

"But look at the veterans. Look at their uniforms. Some have given their blood to wear this medal, and some have not – but all of us are here because we are our 'brother's keeper.'"

"And what is that? What is a 'brother's keeper?'"

"Veterans stand as if at a military funeral: Memorial Day. We hold in our hearts the memory of men whom we served with, with whom we laughed, cried, and yes – whom we bled with. We are the keepers of that memory. So, approach us. Talk to the Veterans. They are here, now. And to veterans: I challenge you to tell that story - that's how that memory is going to be kept alive. We are our brother's keeper."

Then I required God's help. None of the rest of what happened was planned, but what happened next would never leave my memory:

"Now, if there's anyone out there that wears the Purple Heart, please come forward because it will be my honor to give it…if there's anyone who is there, you are welcome to come and receive it from me now."

None of it was planned. I had no idea if anyone would come forward. After a few seconds of silence, dead silence among hundreds on that beautiful spring day, out came a veteran from the Vietnam War. The crowd, seeing all of it, did not break applause for many minutes. It was *incredibly* loud.

But I couldn't hear it really. Soon neither could he. Tears. Up he came and stood at attention in front of me and we saluted each other. "You are your brother's keeper – don't forget that - I said to him. What you have done for America we will never forget." It was simple and difficult; even the hardest heart broke watching the Purple Heart pinned over heart of the veteran who earned it. But while I was thus focused something else happened I did not expect. Up behind him came another much older veteran from World War II with his wife and cane. I only had *one* Purple Heart, and after pinning it upon the Vietnam veteran, he turned around as the village was still clapping louder. He turned, face to face to the older veteran and did not flinch in what he did next. He took it off his chest and in front of the whole world pinned it upon the older veteran – honoring him and honor in turn. It was unforgettable. It could not be better planned but by God himself.

I found out later that the WWII veteran never got the Purple Heart he earned because the grenade he was hit by was thrown two days after the war had officially ended in 1945. *Two days.* That was all that stood between him and the honor he deserved. All those years later and finally he was recognized publicly for something that had been there all along. Remarkable. The whole town saw God at work that day in 2018.

The Purple Heart

★★★★★

2021. The old marine went to the computer and did not stop typing until morning. Exhausted, God had provided a solution, and it was about to be a long - sometimes lonely road where all the Maker could do was to deal with the marine who was fond of excuses. But he kept typing, and in short order it was done, and social media was doing its magic. **The movement to honor the Purple Heart for ALL combat wounds - for combat-incurred Post Traumatic Stress Disorder was born.** The sum of so much life and prayers found purpose in honoring a veteran's legacy...and I knew it would happen. One day it would happen even if I did not live to see it. All Confidence was given that once it was established, it would save lives as a tangible recognition of a daily struggle, but it was much bigger than one man - what one man could manage. What I needed was *completely* outside my ability. What was needed was a miracle.

The plan was simple yet difficult. **The petition had to be signed by a significant number of people - enough to get the attention of the President of the United States to sign**

an executive order. The foremost miracle was convincing the people why it was a necessity. In my mind it was easy, though I knew it would ultimately be up to the President – and why the President? Why not Congress or the Department of Defense?

"The Purple Heart of Merit" was created by our first President George Washington in 1782 to honor wounds received in the defense of America. It was one of our nation's first military honors and its legacy has come all the way from the revolution to current day in the form of the Purple Heart. It was, and it still is the prerogative of the President of the United States. He may honor its meaning any way he wishes – and that is precisely what makes an executive order so elemental.

But other steps would have to be taken…

First, create a new department within the Veterans Administration for the specific purpose of honoring the Purple Heart. **Second**, the said department would verify that the veteran had PTSD *from combat*; established by a certified psychologist. **Third**, in reviewing each case, the veteran must have either a combat ribbon, a campaign ribbon, or both. These satisfied, the veteran would then be sent communication that the United States of America would like to honor the veteran with the Purple Heart for his daily, *living sacrifice* to the Nation. For his daily, *living legacy...*

> *Can you imagine what this would mean to a wayward veteran? Can you imagine what this would mean to him even if he chose never to wear it? Can you imagine what this would mean to the bereaved who are full of unanswered questions?*

In the end all medals are optional to receive, and the veteran would be made aware *if* he desires to be honored - it will be so. Some, no doubt, will decline, but at least the veteran, or the bereaved family will have the knowledge that America is with them even in the darkest hours. Yes, a *tangible* recognition - tangibly honored for an intangible soul. Simple yet difficult. Simple and worth it.

But there was a deeper motivation for the marine typing: *there must be a reason* that some had died for all of this...not the concept of the Purple Heart for all war wounds, but those that had been lost to suicide. Jim and Rus - and a hundred thousand others! He had to believe that they **and** their families were still worth fighting for – that tens of thousands of families everywhere were worth fighting for. The marine was about to start a lifetime pursuit for the Purpose, and it was a long road he didn't mind taking. Enjoy the walk marine...every veteran is worth it.

It wasn't just faith either. All the sudden, research erupted that laid a foundation for the whole movement seen at the QR codes below. In the first ever study of its kind, an examination of ten-thousand combat veterans in 2022 proved that veterans who received the Purple Heart, with or without PTSD, had a 50% less suicide rate than those who did not.[1] In 2011, another study was published in *Dialogues in Clinical Neuroscience* proving that PTSD and TBI symptoms are nearly identical and often co-exist.[2] And, there are **hundreds** of studies in the last few decades that maintain PTSD being a real, legitimate war wound; so it went well beyond faith. It was supported by divinely timed, incredible research.

---

1 Moceri-Brooks, J. (2022). "The Purple Heart and Suicidal Behaviors in Post-9/11 U.S. Army Combat Veterans with a Traumatic Brain Injury: A Mixed Methods Study" (Doctoral dissertation, Duquesne University). Retrieved from https://dsc.duq.edu/etd/2186

2 Richard Bryant (2011) "Post-traumatic Stress Disorder vs Traumatic Brain Injury," Dialogues in Clinical Neuroscience, 13:3, 251-262, DOI: 10.31887/DCNS.2011.13.2/ rbryant. https://doi.org/10.31887/DCNS.2011.13.2/rbryant

The petition on Change.org was working. In a few weeks, five hundred had signed. In another, *over a thousand.* So far, so good. But the marine was busy and fond of excuses. Winter was coming and everything under the sun required attention. Insulation for the house, school for kids, kicking alcohol…and the wind. The wind and -22 of South Dakota felt like death at -50. The petition was in its infancy and there was much to do. The petition needed daily attention, and the excuses started to mount. But all of it was worth it. The little negativity he received was worth it. He decided to put a Purple Heart medal on his very desk to keep him focused, and it worked. In a few years hundreds of calls, emails, meetings, even cursive hand-written letters dented the finish on his desk. Worth it.

But it was hard to see past the dark days…

Lately, the troubled mind had stayed up looking at the stars. Flat on his back, most of the time nothing was in his head. Nights tended to provide a better mood because the work of the day was done, his back could relax - his bloody hands could heal. He did nothing but listen. He knew that God wanted his mind to be clear and meek; wounded and wanting. Wanting an answer but not pushing for it. Wounded enough to keep praying for help. Time slowed down - like the warm summer nights of youth forgetting he was grown. Old. Forgetting his bed, his eyes began to tire. More than one night he spent snoring on the grass when the morning sun hit the frozen dew upon his face. "Just like the old days," he said as the bones cracked up his stiff back.

One thing he discovered in the marines was that *motion equals motivation.* The marine needed to keep moving, keep training because he knew the call would come. After a hundred hours of instruction and thousands of supervised hours, he became a certified peer supporter in combat trauma. A "combat psychologist" so to speak who had also been to hell. He had hoped with some training it would become evident how he could help his peers. He knew a veteran would need to talk and he needed to be ready. It happened weekly, and suddenly complete strangers started to call from all over the United States. He *really* listened to them, and it seemed to help. Though he was trained to be reactive (something that did not suit him), a dozen veterans had his phone number and he always picked up. But he couldn't do it all. It pained him to hear of another veteran gone. He spent years with men in miserable conditions, and he could have hardly known that twenty years later he would desire to see them again especially when they passed. Jim and Rus. He thought if he dug a foxhole in his backyard some might join him. He thought if he bought an Abrams tank some might jump in, but when it came down to it - most were alone, and so was he. Even in the presence of veterans who had been there - he felt alone.

Killing The Spirit

★★★★★

Before a man murders, he *must* kill his soul. He must kill his conscience it before he can kill himself. I understood it, but then again I had never truly been there. Not only that, but it is a fact that other stressors are in play. Veterans are beset by more domestic issues than I can count, and having PTSD from combat just makes it all worse. Some are truly alarming. I know a dozen veterans that are completely taken advantage of by folks that only want them for their pension. One day while walking the halls of the VA, I overheard something deplorable. One gal said to the other, "I just don't make enough to pay the bills."

"Hey, just get yourself a sugar-daddy. They are all over the place here, you might have to wheel them around, but you'll be set!. Medical, dental, and you'll get paid when they croak." The gal was completely serious. It made me sick. The point is, that it is often a succubus in the guise of a loved-one or friend that pushes the veteran to the limit, and his combat scars make it all the worse. And when these veterans protest – "it's because of the war." When they go through three marriages and lose their kids – "it must be the war." When they commit suicide, *of course* it's all blamed on war. It's therefore not hard to see how the veteran feels he has no way out or wants to kill the awful situation by killing himself; and in the end, it is all blamed on a war. Terrible. How could this be addressed? The answer is abstinence, but few believe in abstinence. The answer is faith, but not all have faith. Maybe the answer is a garden, but not all people like gardens. Most people don't like worms.

But what can keep a veteran going?

I knew what kept *me* going: motion and giving. Keeping my hands busy. It validated the daily struggle, at least in my mind, but not everyone was the same. I had to be proactive, and that, by the grace of God, was exactly the solution – for *me*. Helping others **is** rewarding. However, there was no cookie-cutter solution. Every veteran is different; every soul is different. What keeps a soul fighting can be a thousand things and not just confined to the physical world. Honor is found in living for someone else or something else. Sacrifice. To give and give for a greater cause. That's why veterans raise the right hand to serve **for years** even when the going is tough – even if it kills them. Man is imbued with an incredible sense of duty to loved-ones. Indeed, why else does man exist if not for some greater cause?

Then one day I was sent a nastygram. It surprised me when another marine berated the Purple Heart movement in choice language, saying, "don't you water-down my Purple Heart!" *That* surprised me. Some did not agree, and some minds would never be changed. But I had to keep moving because it was the right thing to do. "Do-nothing-ism" was not an option. But for days I ruminated on what the marine said to me. Was he right? He couldn't be. All of it came from Above, but few would believe it. The movement was gaining steam, and a few veterans said basically the same thing, and at the time I had no answer they would accept. It was impossible, even deplorable to some people. Few accept God in the first place much less believe God had a hand in all of it. How would I answer? How should I answer? Should I answer at all? It took no small amount of prayer and knee-time in the garden to figure it out. When it came down to it, I knew it would save lives - indeed, *it already had.* Not long after the petition was created, one veteran told me it gave him "new hope" to be recognized, and that's what it's all about. Acknowledgement. Recognition. Hope. The Purple Heart is sacred, and made more so by tangibly honoring the *daily, living sacrifice* to all veterans who had seen combat. Because they **do** bleed. They bleed on the battlefield, they bleed in attempted suicide, they bleed on the operating table, and they bleed in a thousand ways combat has changed them. What is the Purple Heart if not sacred to all combat wounds? Blood shed yesterday from combat is the same as today - there is no difference. And for those who believe that honoring it for all combat wounds somehow diminishes its worth or the worth of its bearer, the answer is simple - **that** is between you and God.

There is a deep-seated attitude towards psychological wounds, and it is difficult for some to believe they exist, much less be recognized for them. But what we **do** know is that

PTSD is a **real** injury sustained in combat, and NOT the result of a weak or dysfunctional brain, or a weak or dysfunctional soul. Post Traumatic Stress Disorder is the result of a live, vibrant soul exposed to the inhumane, horrific conditions of war. And you don't always know when you see it, and *that* fuels the quiet contempt for psychological wounds of warfare, *especially* in the military. It is often the mental side of a tactical situation, the mental side of battle that is kept quiet, fueling the belief that PTSD is somehow inferior to blood in battle, Traumatic Brain Injury, the operating table - or war itself. The fact is they are *equal.* Each battle wound as sacred as the other. Each is as valid as the other. The question therefore is evident: has America grown enough to recognize all war wounds as sacred? No. The cold truth is *no* - not yet.

The fact is that undiagnosed, untreated PTSD is the number one killer of veterans. They are **three times** more likely to commit suicide than veterans with treatment. Of these, those who live on rural farms and homesteads are **three times MORE** likely to choose suicide. The best, finest Americans, all of which have taken the oath to defend the Constitution, especially the ones who feed America, are fighting a hard fight - and losing. You pass them on the street, and like most everyone else, they suffer in silence. The only difference is that a soul that has seen combat is *much* more afflicted than those who have not. Every veteran, every soul is different especially when it comes to PTSD, and it manifests different in every veteran. The marine understood suffering, and he understood PTSD, but there was something else.

Rabbit Holes

★★★★★

The marine had to take a walk. It wasn't writer's block; it wasn't exhaustion, it was something like soul-searching. He ended up at the town cemetery. He paced the awful, tipped-over headstones, and the nice, polished ones. After an hour he ended up on the grass and thought of nothing. Where they cannot sleep at home, all veterans long for the days they slept on the battlefield. Everyone is too comfortable. Everything is too comfortable, and somehow sleeping on the dirt **is** attractive to veterans who lived for years in the field. Why does the town graveyard seem to be a good place? Who knows. No one goes there really, and it might be nice to sleep on the grass with nothing. Why is it welcoming to sleep on the dead? On them, with them, whatever. What do the stars look like over there? Maybe bring a bottle and sit. Maybe dig a foxhole and get arrested. Maybe talk to valhalla, maybe pray to God. Maybe say nothing and do nothing like a complete freak show. All on a single walk.

Silence. Fireflies. Then my mind flashed back to that day in 2018. "Silence protects loved ones," I said in front of the town. It was the summation of suffering where every veteran chooses silence as a shield. Not for the veteran, but for everyone else. All that claim the tenderest names, those he calls family are *worthy* of a certain level of silence. Silence when a child asks, "how many people have you killed?" Silence when Iraq, or Afghanistan is mentioned. Silence when a loved-one asks, "what's wrong?" when he stares at a red sunrise. All of it. The point is, that it is a veteran's *duty* to shield the innocent from the evil that is combat. The evil that is war. Yes YOU, mother and father, and YOU, sister, brother, daughter, son are protected daily by your veteran: things you should **not** know, and things you should **never** see. In a twisted kind of reality, it is their legacy - it is **your** legacy to be shielded from the things they've seen. THAT is honor. It is a hard sort of honor, but honor nonetheless.

And not all days are bad. Some days we wake up and are ready to take on the world. Some days are perfect. The therapy seems to be working, and the meds seem to be working. The darkness abates after a great night's rest - comatose sleep is best. No dreams, no midnight patrols, no domestic issues; nothing out of the ordinary. Positivity radiates with the sunrise. No. Not all days are bad. But these days are rare. Chasing a perfect night's sleep seems to be combat now. The bed sometimes fights and causes us to toss and turn endlessly like a pig on a spit. We hate it - that sleepless place of defeatism, restlessness; the opposite of peace. Even so, there are good days.

Then, it hits like lightning. At the family barbeque, someone scorched the meat, or someone burnt their arm hair, and his whole world is filled with tanks and explosions. The smell brings him back. Smells always bring us back. The veteran is somewhere else in time, and it is **your** job to cover for him while he needs a minute. Yes YOU. I am talking to loved ones. Learn to recognize when your veterans' energy goes completely off and have his back while he has yours. Yes. It happens *that* fast. Be vigilant. Be ready.

The Purple Heart for ALL Combat Wounds

★★★★★

Was it the answer to kill suicide? For many, yes. Did I believe it? Yes. Would people accept broadening the definition of blood in combat to blood at home *from combat*? Eventually, yes. Would they be able to see that war is a catalyst to veteran suicide? Yes. Even more, would the President of the United States accept it? Most of all, would veterans accept it? Whatever the case, for the marine typing it was **unacceptable** to do nothing. He had to keep moving.

For the marine and his God, doing nothing would be a failure. "Do-nothing-ism" like Dr. Martin Luther King said, where we know the problem and choose to do nothing. Was it a failure to dream of the possible and **not** take steps towards it daily? Maybe not failure, but negligence? Dereliction of duty? The natural extension of faith is to use the gifts one had been given, and it was robbery, a waste of time, a waste of material when they were not used. "Muscular writing" a mentor once said to me, *and I would use it* by God – anything to prevent another suicide.

One night on an online discussion with other combat-scarred veterans, there was a man who was completely stricken with grief. Red-in-the-face, painful grief. His PTSD, all the garbage he picked up in Afghanistan was brought home, and *years* of misery after the war caused his family to leave. They couldn't deal with it. He was alone in the pandemic in front of a bright screen and a pitch-black room so we could barely see him. "It made me lose my family…" he wept, "I lost my family." This was as real as it got when I spoke to veterans. There were two psychologists in the chatroom, and they said nothing. Nothing. What the hell was wrong with them?! There was a great silence when the man kept on weeping. Weeping like his family were dead and there was nothing else in life worth living. Then a veteran spoke up. He said, "I'm going to send up a prayer for you right now. The prayer was heard, and it helped. But in the end, when the chatroom closed, he was alone in that dark place. Alone. God knows what happened to him, but he at least had a number. A single phone number. Sometimes that's all it takes. But it happened, and it stuck enough to be written, and had it **not** been written, no one would know how to help.

Truth Compounded

There is truth in compounded, wasted material. Everyone has gifts and finite time to use them. We ignore each other now more than ever. Need we discuss our technological age where the screen rules, and people are ghosts behind them? Screens are the ultimate distraction that *kills*. Your voice, your gifts, your time become slave to a dopamine machine, and when you are thus absorbed, you become *wasted material.* Wasted gift to someone who really needs you. Your qualities become mute not only to yourself, but everyone around you. This is what kills. It can kill you in mind, spirit, then body. But some wake up. At some point you will become aware of the time you lost - of the opportunities lost, of the people you lost, and grieve the time the screen took from you. You will then take one of two courses: "do-nothing-ism," turn to the screen until you explode, or **own it** and live. Need we discuss what a human being is capable of when his spirit is killed, when his flame goes out and cares for nothing? The truth is, compounded unaddressed sorrows will make any person feel like life is not worth living. Who could tell this man behind a screen "your life is worth living" when his screen goes cold and there's nothing between him and an awful quiet room? How can one say, "live by grace" and not offer him the things he needs to keep living? When someone is all alone – it can truly feel like the end. So, give him or her your number and time and be ready to listen. It will be hard, but that's exactly what they need. And, if they trust you enough in the first place to tell you something sacred, do them honor by never telling another living soul what you've heard. That is honor. It is a hard sort of honor, but honor, nonetheless.

But all the questions swirled up to heaven:

> *I didn't do this...I didn't do that when I should have. I should have...then this, then that. I wasn't there when I should have been. Maybe he would be alive if...maybe if I wasn't so distracted...I failed as a father, a mother...I left, I ran away. I abandoned them...they abandoned me...I should had fought...I should have ran...I hate Iraq, Vietnam, war. It's all because of the war...if it wasn't for me being screwed up...then everyone would be happy. Then this...then that. I am totally screwed up...*

Time is a gift when you live in the present - no man lives to himself.

Mend your fences when they break - tomorrow may never come.

But when a veteran is wounded on the battlefield, he is often shipped off to a place away from his unit against his will. From that hell, he is swept away to a military hospital. Ripped away from his friends, the helicopter lands and the operating table awaits. Pain. *Years* of pain awaits the veteran who is bleeding for his country. Conscious or not, a whole new chapter begins in his life apart his unit – his world, and nothing will ever be the same. He feels very much alone.

He recovers in a room sometimes full of other suffering veterans. Every conceivable wound is nurtured and treated. It may be a limb sacrificed for liberty, a brain injury, or an eye for blindness so others can see. Whatever is treated, they all lay there in a room full of unfamiliar faces. They long for release. "*Anything* but here." Maybe it is going home. Maybe to war again. Back to his unit. Maybe for an honorable discharge. Maybe all of it. Maybe none of it.

Then, the representative makes his appearance. Sometimes it is a President, or a General, or a Senator, and more commonly a captain or a colonel. Tough they dominate the room in every other circumstance; the high-ranking officers stand as a pauper next to the men that bleed. They are immediately taken in by the room they behold - the sight burns in their mind of what true honor is - what true honor looks like. What sacrifice looks like. In politics and normal life, there is no honor outside sacrifice or outside God - None. Politics is devoid of it. Domestic life is normally devoid of it, and only love becomes it; and here is a whole room of those who gave themselves to complete strangers. For you. YOU. Most are Americans, and some are soon to become Americans. All of them have sacrificed for you: a complete stranger.

One by one, the representative takes place by the bedside, and one by one, the veterans are honored with the Purple Heart. It *is* the most sacred recognition in America. It is an honor purchased with sacrifice. Purchased by battle. And yet it is so much more. Though it *is* honor, though it is tangible, though it is fragile, it is **life**. It *becomes* the veteran who bears it. It builds him up, cements his legacy, an American legacy, a badge of *living sacrifice* to the US Constitution, the finest living government man has conceived on this earth. What is the Purple Heart if not honored for **all** combat wounds? Let us honor the daily, living sacrifice of all combat wounded with the most sacred medal of the United States of America.

The prayer was sent up not so long ago, and it was going to be a long road. He asked his Maker for energy, inspiration, patience, wisdom, and so much more. But he also realized he could not do it alone. **You** are needed. You can help by not only signing the petition at the QR code below, but folding it up and keeping it in your wallet or purse wherever you go. When you give it away, fold up another and print a few more. Share the petition and this pamphlet far and wide. Use social media, email, put up fliers at gas stations with the QR code, and most of all, use the gifts you've been given - one day it will save a life. No man lives to himself, and we need each other now more than ever to combat suicide. Send up a prayer. You are the flame that may save a life.

Honor the Purple Heart for ALL Combat Wounds

★★★★★

Veterans are dying of suicide every day. Everyone knows; and no one knows what to do. What can we do?

We have a solution that will save lives.

Whomever you may be, a President, a General, a Senator, a congressman, we need you to act. Veterans need your help. This letter has been in my pocket for you.

Many veterans have severe Post Traumatic Stress Disorder from combat long ago. *From combat.* Not regular service, but *combat* that may have happened years, or decades ago.

America needs to honor them. At this moment in time, The Purple Heart is honored to veterans with wounds of war. It is gotten with sacred blood on the battlefield, and on the battlefield only. From war, and war only.

I, and thousands more argue that blood shed on the operating table, and blood shed in suicide *from combat* is the same now as it was in war: whether it be a day, or thirty years afterward. It makes no difference. Combat incurred PTSD **is** a real war wound.

We propose that the Purple Heart be honored for PTSD from War.

We ask for an Executive Order to be made for this end.

We propose that the Veterans Administration set up a new department explicitly for this purpose.

America must recognize the daily *living* sacrifice of all warriors, or else we will lose them.

Blood shed yesterday is the same as today **if** it stems from combat. This must be so.

This recognition is far more than a medal; *that* is secondary. It is a debt America has to its men and women formally recognized in entirety. A recognition of their daily, *living* sacrifice for this nation; a recognition of their living legacy.

This will change the heart of many, and with Providence, will cause less to take their own lives in the knowledge that America is with them even in the darkest hours.

Please scan and vote YES below. Please forward this as necessary. They need you. We need you. Make this a priority. Do not go to sleep until it is done.

FOR
MILITARY
MERIT

www.ingramcontent.com/pod-product-compliance
Lightning Source LLC
LaVergne TN
LVHW051923051126
851857LV00021B/2118
* 9 7 9 8 9 9 7 3 0 5 8 0 2 *